M. Fry

THE GOLDEN CITY

Books illustrated by Neil Waldman

Nessa's Fish (by Nancy Luenn)

Nessa's Story (by Nancy Luenn)

Mother Earth (by Nancy Luenn)

America the Beautiful (by Katharine Lee Bates)

The Gold Coin (by Alma Flor Ada)

THE GOLDEN CITY

JERUSALEM'S 3,000 YEARS

WRITTEN AND ILLUSTRATED BY

NEIL WALDMAN

ATHENEUM BOOKS FOR YOUNG READERS

Atheneum Books for Young Readers
An imprint of Simon & Schuster Children's Publishing Division
1230 Avenue of the Americas, New York, NY 10020
Copyright © 1995 by Neil Waldman
All right reserved including the right of reproduction in whole or in part in any form.
Designed by Ann Bobco
The text of this book is set in New Baskerville
The illustrations are rendered in watercolor and colored pencils.
Manufactured in the U.S.A.
10 9 8 7 6 5 4 3 2 1

Library of Congress Cataloging-in-Publication Data
Waldman, Neil.
The golden city : Jerusalem's 3,000 years / written and illustrated by Neil Waldman.
p.   cm.
ISBN 0-689-80080-0
1. Jerusalem—History—Juvenile literature. 2. Jerusalem—Religion—Juvenile literature.
[1. Jerusalem—History.] I. Title.
DS109.9.w27 1995   95-2137
956.94'42—dc20   CIP
                                                            AC

ISBN: 0-689-80080-0

For Kathy Moses, friend of my soul

The Eastern Road to Jerusalem winds its way up from the lowest spot on earth, a blazing cauldron known as the Dead Sea. It climbs through the rocky hillsides, higher and higher above the desert, until cypress and olive trees dot the landscape. Soon the air grows cooler and forests of pine appear on the slopes. Then, high atop a stony hill, you can see the walls of the city, with gold and silver domes, and minarets and towers sparkling behind the massive stone ramparts.

Once within the gates, you walk along ancient cobbled alleyways, unaware of the many layers of history that lie hidden beneath your feet. You step on the very stones where, a thousand years ago, a young crusader lay bleeding, slain by an arrow that had just pierced his armor. You turn a corner and pass a doorway where, nearly two millennia earlier, a great prophet discussed the future of humanity with his disciples. You climb up onto the city walls and look out over a valley where, three

thousand years before, a young boy slew a giant warrior with a slingshot.

This is Jerusalem, where civilization after civilization has come and gone, each arriving in victory and vanishing in defeat. For over three thousand years armies have laid siege to the city walls, breached them, and destroyed all that stood within. Then, upon the rubble, they built their new cities. And so over the centuries, Jerusalem has risen higher and higher, layer upon layer, civilization upon civilization.

Today, as you walk through the city, you will find the remains of all these civilizations. The skyline is an architectural patchwork of many eras. Near the Western Wall, you can peer down a dark shaft and see the striations of the many cities of antiquity, piled one upon the other. And on the eastern side of the city there is a place where you can climb down into caverns beneath the ground and walk through the remains of these ancient cities.

Atop the highest hill

It all started when Moses came down from Mount Sinai carrying the tablets of the law. He announced to his people, the Israelites, that God had given the tablets to him, and that they were the laws God intended them to follow. They placed the tablets in a carved box and carried it with them as they wandered for many centuries. They took it into many battles, believing that the awesome power of God lay within the box, making their armies invincible. Once the Philistines captured the tablets and the Israelites went to war to retrieve them.

When David became king he took Jerusalem from the Jebusites, and the centuries of wandering came to an end. He made Jerusalem his capital city and found a place for the tablets of the law atop a rock within the city walls. This rock, known as Mount Moriah, was believed to be the place where God had commanded Abraham to sacrifice his son, Isaac. For the first time, the tablets had a permanent resting place and the Jewish people had a spiritual home. Still within the nomad's tent that had protected them for centuries, the tablets were taken to Mount Moriah and securely placed upon the rock. Great festivities were held and King David danced wildly through the streets.

David's city, 975 B.C.E.

When David's son Solomon became king, he made Jerusalem
the showpiece of his expanding empire. He fortified the walls of
the city to protect the many new structures springing up within.
He built a royal palace, and a magnificent stone temple on

Mount Moriah to replace the nomad's tent that had housed the tablets of the law for so long. The splendor of the city attracted visitors from faraway lands. On holidays, people from all over the empire came to pray and celebrate in their spectacular capital.

Solomon's city had stood for nearly four hundred years when Nebuchadnezzar, king of Babylon, attacked and overran Jerusalem. His armies leveled all the beautiful buildings, destroyed the temple, and carried the people of Israel in chains back to Babylon. In Babylon the Jews dreamed of returning and rebuilding their beloved home. In Psalm 137, written in Babylon, the longing of the Jews for their homeland is revealed:

> *How shall we sing the Lord's song in a strange land?*
> *If I forget thee, O Jerusalem, let my right hand lose its cunning.*

For fifty years the city that had for so long been one of the world's great wonders lay in ruin. Broken stones and charred wooden beams littered the streets. Lizards and snakes slithered through the bleached bones of those who had died in battle. Thorny trees and cactus grew up amid the desolation.

When the Jews began returning from Babylon, they were determined to rebuild their city. Their loving hands slowly rekindled Jerusalem's golden light. After seven long years of labor King Solomon's great temple stood once again high atop Mount Moriah.

Two centuries later the mighty armies of Alexander the Great conquered most of the known world and the land of Judea became part of the Greek empire. Jerusalem was taken without a battle, leaving it unharmed. For many generations the Greeks ruled Jerusalem peacefully, until Antiochus Epiphanes became king and everything changed. He made practice of the Jewish religion illegal. He destroyed the sacred Torah scrolls in the temple and began sacrificing pigs at the altar. Jews were forced to eat pork and practice the Greek religion.

A group of Greek soldiers entered a mountain village near Jerusalem, with orders to force the Jews to bow down to a Greek statue. An old Jewish priest named Mattathias became enraged and he slew the first Jew who stepped forward. He then killed the Greek commander and smashed the statue with his sword.

Mattathias and his five sons, the Maccabees, escaped into the surrounding hills and began organizing a revolt. With their intimate knowledge of the terrain, the Maccabees and their supporters smashed the Greeks again and again, escaping to the caves and wadis of the Judean hills.

As word of their success spread through the land, their tiny army multiplied until it was a great fighting force. After several decisive battles the Maccabees succeeded in driving the Greeks from their land.

They returned to Jerusalem and were saddened by what they found. The temple had been desecrated, the gates burned, and much of the city destroyed. Thousands of people joined in a massive rebuilding and the temple was rededicated. In memory of that joyous day, the festival of Chanukah came into being.

The Judean hills,
where the Maccabees hid

The new Jewish nation was barely a hundred years old when the mighty armies of Rome laid siege to the city. They surrounded the walls and attacked with giant stone throwers, assault towers, and battering rams. The Jews fought on for three months, but finally the walls were breached and the city destroyed.

The Romans appointed Herod king of Judea and he began another rebuilding campaign that recalled the days of Solomon. A wide avenue crossed the city center, with great columns at either side. New buildings sprang up everywhere: magnificent palaces, a sports stadium, luxurious bath houses, amphitheaters, beautiful gardens, and bubbling fountains. Herod then rebuilt Solomon's temple, larger and more magnificent than before.

Herod's city, 34 B.C.E.

It was during this time that a young man called Jesus of Nazareth came upon the scene, and changed human history. As a boy, his parents brought him to Jerusalem every year to celebrate Passover. As he grew he was moved by the suffering of the common people, and he began preaching his doctrine of love, brotherhood, and forgiveness. As an adult, he returned to Jerusalem with his disciples, making the same Passover pilgrimage he had made as a boy. He knew full well that he was placing himself in danger, for the priests and the Roman rulers were worried that his followers would grow in number and threaten their authority. He was captured and sentenced to death by crucifixion, which was the Roman method of execution. After his death, his disciples spread Jesus' teachings out from Jerusalem, to the farthest reaches of the empire, and eventually to almost all the nations of the earth.

*The Church
of Mary Magdalene*

*The Franciscan Convent
of the Flagellation*

As the years passed, Roman oppression increased, and the Jews revolted again, and then again. Twice they drove the Romans from Jerusalem and established their own government. They held power for several years, but when the Romans recaptured the city for the second time, they determined never to allow the Jews to revolt again. On the ninth day of Av, the same day that centuries earlier the Babylonians had destroyed Solomon's temple, the Roman legions overran the city and burned it down. They stormed the streets, killing all the men, women, and children they could find. They scoured the countryside, rounding up Jews and sending them to Rome in chains, where they were paraded through the streets as part of a great victory procession. They leveled Jerusalem, attempting to erase it forever from the pages of history. Atop the rubble, they built a new Roman city which they named Aelia Capitolina.

The Jews were scattered, sold as slaves throughout the empire and destined to wander the face of the earth for centuries. From country to country they passed, staying until they were evicted, suffering greatly along their endless road. During these times of great pain, they passed their memories of the Golden City from generation to generation. They told their children stories of the Maccabees and the Temple of Solomon. They never abandoned the dream that someday they would return home. At the end of the Passover each year, Jews around the world would proclaim, "Next year in Jerusalem."

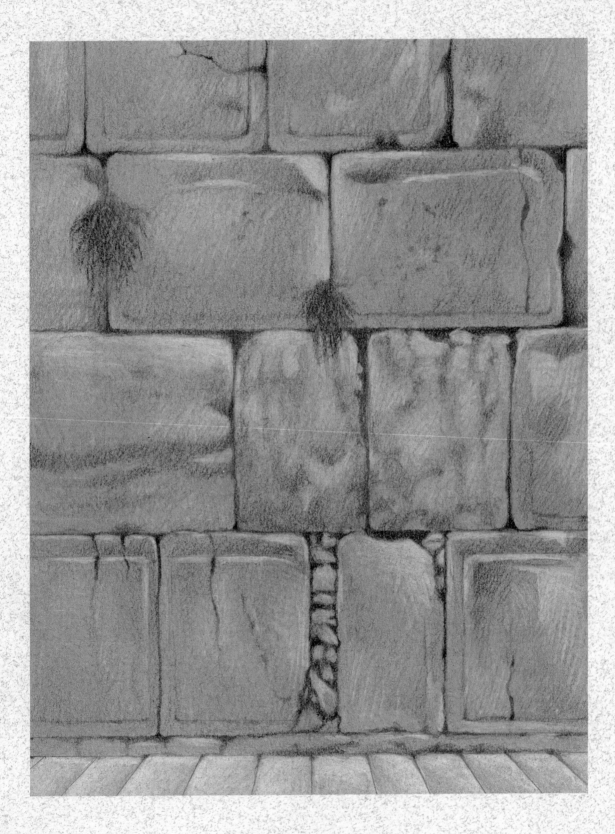

*Under the rule
of Christian Rome,
521 C.E..*

After four centuries of Roman rule, when Christianity became the official religion of the empire, Jerusalem became the holy city of Christians as well as Jews. Many churches were built on places where Jesus had walked and the face of the city changed once again.

In the seventh century, great armies of Bedouin horsemen swept out of the Arabian Peninsula and conquered a huge area that extended from Spain to India. The land of Judea, with Jerusalem at its center, was now part of the great Arab empire. The Arabs believed that the prophet Muhammad had ascended to heaven riding a magnificent stallion that flew up from Mount Moriah, and Jerusalem became holy to the followers of a third great religion, Islam. The Arabs filled the city with beautiful houses of prayer called mosques. They allowed the Christian inhabitants of the city to continue practicing their religion, and they welcomed the Jews back, as well.

The Dome of the Rock,
the great mosque
on Mount Moriah

The northern walls

For more than four centuries the Muslims ruled peacefully in Judea until massive waves of Christian armies descended on the city from Europe. These were the crusaders—knights and commoners spurred on by the Catholic pope Urban II. The crusaders were determined to free their holy city from the Muslims. After a month of fighting, they broke into the city and massacred all the Muslims and Jews inside. As the crusaders charged through the streets, the last living Jews fled to a synagogue. The soldiers surrounded the building and set it on fire, burning all the people alive. Two days later they marched through the city to the Church of the Holy Sepulchre, which stood on the hill where Jesus was crucified. There they knelt and prayed, thanking Jesus for their victory.

The crusaders remained in power for less than a hundred years. They were defeated by Saladin, a powerful Armenian ruler from Damascus, who restored Muslim rule to the city. For the next several centuries, a succession of Muslim rulers remained in power.

The Temple Mount under Muslim rule, 1527 C.E.

Crosses carved by medieval pilgrims in the Church of the Holy Sepulchre

Throughout this period, Jews continued to trickle back into Jerusalem. First under the Egyptian Mameluks, and then under the Ottoman Turks, the Jewish community grew.

Toward the end of the nineteenth century, anti-Semitism in Europe made life there unbearable, and many Jews began to look eastward to their ancient homeland as a solution to their problems. Thousands of Jews arrived each year until, by the beginning of the twentieth century, the majority of Jerusalem's population was Jewish. In 1948 the state of Israel was established, with Jerusalem as its capital. Actually, the Jewish state included only half the city, for the new border ran right through the city center, with Israel possessing the western half of the city and Jordan possessing the eastern half. In the Six Day War of 1967, the Israeli army captured the Jordanian side of the city, and the Jewish government annexed it. Today Jerusalem remains in Jewish hands.

The Tomb of Zachariah, the prophet

Just as in centuries past, thousands of people from faraway places come to visit Jerusalem each year. They are drawn by the splendor of the place, the magnificent domed mosques and the narrow alleyways, the delicate carvings and the massive ramparts, the ancient shrines and modern museums. But hidden beneath all these visible things is the mysterious feeling that, as you pass

through the city gates, you are actually drifting back past the days of fabled knights and prophets, to the time when a young boy slew a giant with a slingshot.

Jerusalem today

JERUSALEM, 3,000 years of history

B.C.E.

1004	King David establishes Jerusalem as the capital of Israel
961	King Solomon begins building the First Temple
587	Destruction of the city by the Babylonians
537	Return of the Jews from Babylon
332-167	Rule of the Greeks
167	Maccabean War of Liberation
63	The Romans capture Jerusalem
37-34	The rule of King Herod, building of the Second Temple

C.E.

33	The Crucifixion of Jesus
66-70	The Jewish War against the Romans
70	The fall of Jerusalem; the destruction of the Second Temple
135	Total destruction of the city; the building of a new city named Aelia Capitolina; the exile of the Jews
324	Beginning of the Christian period
326	Building of the Church of the Holy Sepulchre
638	Muslims capture Jerusalem
691	Dome of the Rock completed
1099	Crusader capture of Jerusalem
1187	Saladin recaptures the city from the crusaders
1250-1517	Rule of the Mameluks
1517-1917	Rule of the Ottoman Turks
1917-1948	British occupation
1948	Birth of the modern state of Israel; the city is divided
1967	Israeli troops capture the eastern side of the city during the Six Day War